I0901743

IDENTITY

FORDHAM UNIVERSITY PRESS NEW YORK 2015

COMMONALITIES

Timothy C. Campbell, series editor

IDENTITY

Fragments, Frankness

JEAN-LUC NANCY

Translated by François Raffoul

This book was originally published in French as Jean-Luc Nancy, *Identité: Fragments, franchises* © Éditions Galilée, 2010.

Library of Congress Control Number: 2014944566

Printed in the United States of America
17 16 15 5 4 3 2 1
First edition

CONTENTS

Preface to the English-Language Edition vii

0 Fragments 1
1 Causes and Consequences 3
2 *Gros Rouge* 7
3 Identity Is Not a Figure 9
4 Frankly 13
5 Absolute 17
6 Who? 21
7 Why Speak of Identity? 25
8 Peoples 29
9 Nations 33
10 Empires 39
11 Identities, Intimacies 41

Notes 43

PREFACE TO THE ENGLISH-LANGUAGE EDITION

This book was written in circumstances determined by a French context. It is thus important to clarify the situation in which it was published, particularly for the English-speaking reader, five years later. The stakes of its theme, however—the identity of a people or a nation, and identity in general (let us say, of a "subject")—are by no means circumscribed by this situation. On the contrary, we are immersed in an effervescence of identity claims of all kinds (national, ethnic, religious, sexual, cultural, and so forth) through which nothing is more in question than the very notion and thinking of *identity*. To be perhaps too concise, this concept seems to have lost all vitality: all plasticity, differentiation, and complexity. This more or less generalized petrification is such that a reflection on identity cannot be limited to the French situation.

The following pages, whether a book, a polemical essay or a pamphlet, were born from a feeling of anger. In 2009, the president of the French Republic, Nicolas Sarkozy, decided to launch a large popular debate on "French identity." Conferences, meetings, and debates were supposed to be organized throughout the country around the question of "French identity." The reason for this quite singular initiative was given by the President himself: "As a result of our neglect, we have arrived at a point where we no longer know who we are," he declared on November 12, 2009.

What "neglect" was he referring to? It is both easy and difficult to answer: easy if one thinks here of the most stereotyped discourse of the nostalgic right-wing, namely that there was a France once, primordial, essential, with a proper, inalienable history and even a substance, which we have eventually forgotten by exposing ourselves to multiculturalism, globalization, and so forth. But difficult too if one thinks that Sarkozy was also posing as a champion of the free-market philosophy that would be most suited to erase borders, extend markets, increase exchange, and measure identities in terms of bank accounts.

This blatant contradiction was the first cause for anger. Another reason was provided by the political reasons that led to the invention of the "debate on national identity": it was a matter of regaining ground on the extreme-right, not in order to defeat it but rather to take its place by showing that one could give new life to what is formulated in the program of the National Front in this way: "France is an old human land [terre], heir to several of the greatest civilizations in History, which it unified in an original culture."

The ridiculousness of this declaration—which could apply to other nations, if not all, and which thus declares nothing—should disqualify it from the outset. However, the "neglect" deplored by Sarkozy indeed referred to the spirit of that declaration if not to its letter. In order to appropriate the grandiose and ridiculous overtones of the far-right celebration, it was necessary to indulge also in the denouncing of a loss—abandonment, oblivion, betrayal, and degradation of what one supposes "France" must have been.

One must indeed suppose that such a thing as "France" did exist at one time if one wishes that it exists again. The logic of renewal, rebirth or restoration always involves a fantastical or imaginary logic. In the nineteenth century—when "nationalities" (which was the prevalent word at the time) flourished—some French people fantasized that the Gallic language was the original language of humanity. (The very notion of an original language was already itself a phantasm.) However, "nationalities" were formed in Europe in a quite ambivalent manner: on the one hand, it was a matter of freeing oneself from imperial and post-feudal powers in the name of democratic ideals, and on the other hand one had to give a political content (in the sense of the sovereign State) to geo-cultural configurations that until then were not constituted according to national figures. Further, national entities nonetheless often allowed important cultural and economic diversities to exist within them. More than one European country bears the marks of this, brought back today by the general weakening of nation-states and of techno-financial sovereignty.

The United States of America was founded on an identity that consisted entirely (at least from a moral and juridical point of view) in its own declaration, a declaration itself drawing from a divine source. This is no doubt what allowed both identification with the federal State (through, on the one hand, four years of civil war and seven hundred thousand dead, and, on the other hand, the progressive erasure of . . . the identities? existences? presences? chances? of Native Americans) and the typically "American" concern for a representation of itself, for an "American figure" as well as its questioning, doubting, and parody. But in this way, American identity became indissociable from a capacity to represent itself as the supranational identity of a "democracy" destined to dominate the world.

The European concern with retrieving supposedly lost identities no doubt testifies either to the fear of losing a dominant position, or to the desire of acquiring such a position. Such a region in Europe may wish to acquire its independence in order to give a symbolic status to its economic capacities. On the contrary, a nation such as France deplores the economic weakness that damages and degrades the prestigious image it had been accustomed to present to the world.

In any case, the identity one claims, whether it is supposedly lost, ignored, or self-declared, implies a kind of fundamental distraction—if not denial—with respect to the difference with itself that an identity cannot eliminate without becoming a monolithic block.

The identical is the same as itself, and in order to be so it must reduce to the "same" the indefinite diversity, heterogeneity, and alterity in which and through which this "same" exists. Not only must Hegelian self-consciousness come out of itself to return to itself, but a careful reading of Hegel "himself" could show that this return to itself is necessarily infinite (an infinite which is also intertwined with finitude). The identical never comes to *itself*. It can always presuppose *itself* but its presupposition always throws it further back or further ahead (beyond its two-fold "end").

The *selfhood* of a people is even more problematic (if one can express it in this way) than that of an individual, if we can trust this notion of "individual," which is only operative in the context of a particular culture. This is why the words *people*, *nation*, *country*, and *community* have the complex, undetermined, or even contradictory senses that we know them to have, and why they are as dangerous to use as difficult to simply dispense with. The instance of the "I" that utters itself does not fail, even if it is empty and knows itself to be so. The "we" cannot ignore that it is only instantiated through projection or proxy. Its enactment—its speaking—demands a situation in which projection, proxy, delegation, or representation are, as it were, suspended for an instant. This instant could be called *sovereign* with good reason—and it is indeed from this perspective that modern political sovereignty would have or could have been conceived. It is in such an instant that the Preamble to the Constitution of the United States was pronounced, according to the quite singular and perhaps untenable syntax that says: "*We, the People of the United States.*" But in that founding moment the vacuity of the instant, or, more exactly, the distance internal to the instant through which the statement differs from the enunciation, can only result in making the very thing that is being affirmed tremble.

To return to the French context mentioned above: the result is that when a State decides to organize a debate on national identity, it places itself in a perilous position: It proposes to administer a general discussion on the nature and characteristics of the people or of the nation, while it is their institutional representative. Perhaps it puts itself in danger, for the people could disintegrate in the debate and undermine the State's *raison d'être*. Perhaps also it presupposes—a presupposition on national presupposition—that there will be no disintegration but rather the exclusion of a few elements deemed not to conform to the retrieved identity.

Nothing of this kind formally occurred, for the French did not welcome Sarkozy's initiative warmly. Many of them, no doubt, saw its grotesque or pathetic character, including perhaps even the most nationalistic and identity-obsessed. For everyone knows or senses that an identity does not debate about itself and that when it feels the need to affirm itself it is necessarily already at odds with itself.

The translator is grateful to David Pettigrew for his expert advice in the translation of this Preface.

Supposing that identity itself had its relations of uncertainty, the faith that we still place in it could be but the reflection of a state of civilization whose duration will have been limited to a few centuries.

—Claude Lévi-Strauss, Preface to *L'Identité* (1974–75),
edited by Claude Lévi-Strauss

I was I was not who was not was not who.

—William Faulkner, *The Sound and the Fury*

0

FRAGMENTS . . .

. . . yes, stemming from my astonishment: The state of which I am a citizen is launching a national debate on national identity.[1] Has this identity been lost? Has it become decidedly too indecisive? Could it be in danger? But the state is only ever the instrument of the nation: It is not its role to define, and even less to constitute, the identity of the nation. Furthermore, since the only purpose of this initiative is to close the ranks of those who fear for the identity of said identity—the color of one's skin, one's accent, language, and religion—and since at the same time it is a matter of comforting and informing those who wish to claim this nationality that they will be certified by this identity, the entire operation is turning in a circle.

Could it be that the question of national identity is turning, and turning out badly? But do we even know what we are talking about? This was the source of my initial astonishment: that terms as loaded as "identity" and "nation," freighted with—at least—half a century of philosophical, psychoanalytic, ethnological, sociological, and political questioning, could be so blithely thrown around as objects of "debate." Can one imagine a cabinet member, that is to say, an administrator, in charge of managing these concepts and these questions?[2]

Hence these few fragments, hastily written, simply in order not to turn in circles.

They can also be read as offering some preliminary reflections indispensable to any account of the tectonic movements and metamorphoses that today affect alleged "national identities," here as elsewhere.

1

CAUSES AND CONSEQUENCES

We must first make a strong and clear statement, even a violent one if necessary, regarding the perpetual oscillation of causes and effects between assertions from the Right (these people[1] do not want to let themselves be integrated into the national identity) and arguments from the Left (the conditions they are faced with do not even allow them to claim an identity).

We must first make a clear and unequivocal statement, by refusing arguments that deny the most visible causality: Yes, without work, without good places to live, but only those subproducts of an urbanization without urbanity, with no development other than that conceived by patching together obsolete models, it is impossible even to consider a horizon of "identity," even when one desires precisely that. It is thus normal that one finds refuge in small separated identities, overidentified through their separation, hardened, and exacerbated.

It is not a question here of humanitarian compassion or of dissolution into psychosociological relativism, which have rightly been questioned in the conformism of the beautiful souls on the Left. We are not in the beautiful soul, but instead in the damaged body:

a body damaged by unemployment and urban ghettos, by drugs and alcohol, by mindless television, and dull-witted preachers.

Let us be deliberately simplistic: Either there is work, or there isn't. If there is a structural necessity making it such that there is no work—or very little—one must say so and give an account of what the structure produces. If, on the contrary, there can be work—but in a reformed, if not transformed, structure (organization of capital, meaning or direction of "growth," energy needs)—then one must make it happen. But either way, it will be necessary to make room for what is irreducible: not work, nor capital, but people, all of us together.

Then one must further take a stand and refuse the notion that what comes from structure can be imputed to "cultures" or to "mentalities," not to mention racial stereotypes. For effects of structure take place everywhere and affect everyone. Probably more than other European countries, France is sensitive to the ongoing mutation of European civilization, because for a long time it has claimed to be, within Europe, one of its better defined figures—if not the very figure of the realized "nation" (the Republic). It thus suffers more, also, from this movement regarding which one does not fully know whether it is in the process of ripping out all the barriers that still held back the flood or whether it will reverse or divert the inundation.

In short, it is not "national identity"—whether French or not—that is threatened by other identities, but all "identities" that are undergoing a general disidentification of what we used to call "civilization."

Of course, there are here and today, as elsewhere and as always, people who do not want to work or who seek profits more advantageous than those of paid labor. Nonetheless, for drugs or arms dealing to take on the dimensions that we are seeing today, they must be not only accepted but also called for by an entire social, cultural, moral, even international context. It is not the dealers who create the appetite for what they deal, but the other way around. It is not the gangs and the mafias that destabilize a society: It is a destabilized society that gives them an open space in which to operate.

2

GROS ROUGE

The better-informed newspapers reported a statement from the president to his cabinet ministers, in the context of the presentation of the main goals of the two programs for the regional elections of March 2010 and for the great debate on "national identity" that was about to be launched (in November 2009): "*What I want is some* gros rouge[1] *that leaves a stain.*"[2]

One could not state it any better. The *gros rouge* that leaves a stain, the overripe camembert, and the supposedly Gallic *coq* standing on so many bell towers do indeed constitute undeniable markers of identity of the French nation. Or at least of that French nation that for a good century has been resting in cartons full of images irremediably threatened with disintegration and mold. (One will object that the *gros rouge*—adapted, for a great quantity was needed—was the wine of the trenches. Precisely: Nations destroyed each other while destroying the stomachs of their soldiers.)

In 1957, Roland Barthes could write: "To believe in wine is a coercive collective act. A Frenchman who kept this myth at arm's length would expose himself to minor but definite problems of integration, the first of which, precisely, would be that of having to explain his attitude."[3] This is why anyone who calls for a *gros rouge* identity does not have to explain himself and makes himself understood perfectly well.

Unfortunately for the president, French winegrowers have managed in the last twenty years to bring about quite a remarkable transformation of the most ordinary products. Under the twofold pressure of foreign competition and evolving taste (globalization, socialization within consumer society, everything is contained in this microcosm), the *gros rouge* has actually disappeared. Or at least it has disappeared from view, since it still exists for people who have no money and who know how to find it on the bottom shelves where it is hidden.

If the *gros rouge* that leaves a stain is still a feature of French identity, it is thus at best a past identity, belonging to the past, and at worst it is the identity of the most impoverished.

But there is better, or worse: The *gros rouge* that leaves a stain does indeed stain, as its name indicates, and these stains can be washed out only with difficulty, if at all. But we must also recall that the stain it leaves—or used to leave—is never really red, or even any shade of red one might imagine. Its stains are a purplish blue, or a dark purple, with almost brown flecks—in short, its stains are of such a peculiar determination that a specific word is often associated with it, the word *vinasse*, or plonk. This word designates a very bad wine, of course, but it has also been used to indicate a color or an odor.

What remains of that presidential intention? Some *vinasse* stains on a shirt, on a table, and perhaps—why not?—a few drunks on the floor or stumbling out of the bar.

3

IDENTITY IS NOT A FIGURE

The project of having the population of a country hold an official debate about its own identity is one that initiates a deadly process. The inevitable result will be—in truth, it already is from its very announcement—a mark of obsolescence, if not of death properly speaking, with respect to the country in question, to this "identity" whose nature was sought. For other results, one would need to imagine a radicality and a breadth to this debate such that its very terms can be put into question, displaced, or subverted: "identity," then, and "French." This is impossible, it will be said: One would then exit the limits of the project's designs.

And what is the design of this project? It is the schema of an identity that would in some sense be given, received, recognizable, and subject to analysis. One does not ask whether it is appropriate, and to what extent, and how, to speak of a French identity; one asks in what it consists, what it is made of, what it can demand—and consequently also what it has the right to demand for someone to be integrated into it, to be assimilated into it, to become a subject of it (to become a "subject" of French sovereignty in both senses of the word "subject": to submit to the sovereign, while being a fraction of it—roughly, about 1/65,000,000th of the French population).

One must suppose that it is a given, under the implicit conditions of this project of a debate, that one does not expect that some type of "blood and soil" would be the ground of said identity. We believe we are vaccinated against this virus. Let us admit this for the sake of argument, but it is nonetheless the case that the expression "French identity" by itself harbors an invitation, perhaps even an incitement, to entertain something like the French "land," and, on this land, something like a lineage or a "family" with the "ancestors" that we attempted in the past to identify (we were here way back then!) as the Gauls, in order to avoid being classified under the Germanic identity of the Franks whose name we bear.

Thus we have taught "our ancestors the Gauls" to a few generations of Occitans, Alsatians, Bretons or Basques, Senegalese, Malagasy, or Indochinese (all nominal identities that would require a precise examination) with such somnambular diligence that this textbook expression has become a formula for mocking the colonizer's zeal before the memory of the colonized transmitted this irony to the young generations of its children born in twentieth-century France, who now use the term "Gauls" to put down their peers whose forebears were the colonizers. This is an admirable return of an identity fantasized as a vindictive discrimination of former "niggers," "burnous," or "Chinks," or the more recent "blacks" or "beurs"—not to mention the "wops," "polacks," or "boches."

The *boches* have disappeared. The blacks and *reubeus* are still here, and many others, mixed with the Gauls.[1] We know well that they are the problem and that they are the ones who must be brought into the identity in question.

But here already is the problem: An identity is not something one enters, nor is it something one dresses oneself in, and one cannot identify with one (assuming there is any sense in treating it as an entity or a figure) without at the same time modifying it, modalizing it, perhaps transforming it. Identities are never purely stable, nor simply plastic. They are always metastable.

They are metastable because the strength of an identity is not to stabilize itself around itself in a perpetual imitation. This is perhaps what France has too easily believed, on the basis of the strength of having been recognized for a long time—with good reason—as a great figure. But identity is not a figure. An identity is something more subtle, more delicate, and more evasive. Its force lies in displacing, in changing figures.

This is why a strong "national identity" would not propose to debate about what it is, as if it were a matter of analyzing a tableau. It invents another tableau, a new scene, and new characters.

The first question that comes to mind as a way to open—or to close—the debate is necessarily this one: Why then is it French identity alone that proposes such a debate about itself?

France belongs to a Europe in which it is not alone in inquiring about these mutations of populations, of representations, mentalities, ways of life that are also, or will eventually be, mutations of identity. The trouble is that Europe no longer has an identity.

It seems more or less possible to identify several Europes in history: the Europe of cathedrals, the Europe of universities, the Europe of Enlightenment, the Europe of nationalities and of the conquering bourgeoisie, the Europe of the workers' movement. Now ever since all these Europes disfigured themselves in the trenches, in fascisms, in ideological camps and glaciations, "Europe" has become once more the name of a terrified nymph swept up in waves that threaten to drown whatever identity it still has.

Let us note here that the Europes just evoked and roughly identified—or at least configured, combined, coalescent—were all composed of Germans and French, of English, Austrians, Italians, Spaniards, Dutch, Swedes, also Poles and Czechs, to go no farther with a list that could become quite long. What was proper to these Europes was the very combination of such a multiplicity. It was made of what one called at times, precisely, the "character" of "peoples" whose distinctive features were at once linguistic, cultural, and spiritual, of mentalities and traditions.[2] A time came when this fertile ground was exploited by nationalisms. But I do not think that one spoke of "identity" before adding to it "national": The words "character," "nature," and "temperament" were gentler, less rigid, less policing, and less political.

Further, generally "identity" is a word that is used mostly within the logical, philosophical, and judicial domains with the sense of a permanent unity identical to itself. It thus became in the nineteenth century an administrative term—a document, a nameplate, an identity card. It entered into broader usage only when its logical core—the identical as such, the x = x—became the site of a general interrogation whose model was: What if x *differed* from x?—an individual, an ensemble, any type of unity. But one could say that it remained an abstract word, stuck in its equality with itself, opening up with difficulty to that internal alterity that thought, since Hegel, slowly opened within it—in that for Hegel the identity of the identical is only an "abstract identity." Leibniz already felt the need to assert that there are no two concrete identical (indiscernible) beings in the world: The rigidity of the concept was being felt.

4

FRANKLY

A frank identity: an identity that is clear, distinct, indubitable, even emphasized and, further, declared, open, exposing itself with a resolute sincerity. In order to present oneself, to display "who" one is—substantially so, apart from numbers and the codes of the administrative control of identity—one must have a certain frankness of speech, a *franc-parler* in which one speaks one's mind. And one needs no less frankness to tell someone how one "sees" them. This resolute sincerity is possible only through the free or affranchised character of the one who identifies himself or herself in this way: *franc* in the sense of *franc-bourgeois*[1] or of a *franc-tireur* [maverick or free lance], subject to no authority and to no tutelage, free and *franc du collier* [frank, direct], as one used to say.

It is because he or she is *frank* in the second sense that he or she can be so in the first sense. His or her independence gauges and engages his or her sincerity, which is not an absence of dissimulation but the expression of the fact that he or she is free from all dependency: from all provenance, reference, allegiance.

No doubt this also means that the affranchisement can become entirely internal—that I can affirm myself while under a threat that would seek to extort something else from me. In the end, it was dying people who cried out "*Vive la France*!" as they fell under the bullets at the Mont Valérien fortress. In the end, it is a gaze incapable of speech that stares at the SS—or some other executioner, signifying to them that it is offering them, whole, frank, forever withdrawn—thus inaccessible—the identity that the other sought to reduce. If we say, by convention, that murder terminates a life whereas an execution seeks to annihilate an identity, then in all forms of execution we will find this affirmation that, from the victim, rebounds toward the executioner: Here I am, forever unassailable.

This affirmation is at the basis of all affirmation of identity. Affranchisement and independence are deeper than my dependency on myself (my taste, my desires, and my fears). They are set infinitely far back, at a place where "I" am before being anyone. This most certainly does not mean that I do not recognize or incorporate in my identity more than one trait that comes from elsewhere, from so many elsewheres and so many identities just as distinct. But the point is the place from where identity—mine, his, hers, yours—utters itself, declares itself. The *frank* point of an "I am" that, before any qualification or attribution, enunciates—which amounts to giving—the condition of possibility of any statement of the type "I am *x*," where *x* does not at all designate first the unknown that will be resolved by the particulars of all sorts (social, psychological) but is rather a precondition: "I am frank; I say in all independence that and how I can say that I am (that I identify myself)."

History has taught us all too well about the extorted identities—the "I am Christian" or the "I am a resistant," to mention two examples of declarations often obtained through violence or ruse. Whether their content is true or false matters little since one must in each case find out why, how, and for what purpose the declaration has been made. But it does reveal this: When it is not first of all a question of providing proof, of giving references, then *frankness* [*franchise*] is fully in play; I assure that I am free to affirm who I am. No statements made by another can do anything to change this. The *reservatio mentalis* used by the Marranos, and, like them but in a less systematic way, by many who "converted" out of necessity, may have seemed, in other contexts, a Jesuitical ruse; it nevertheless expresses this fact that there is somewhere an inalienable *franc-penseur* [free thinker] who is irreducible, except by executing him or her, which suppresses the question raised. There is a *zona franca,* or free zone, governed by no authority, not even that of my will or my desire, a zone about which I can say nothing in terms of "identification" (characterization, attributions), but about which I know that it is, prior to me, that on the basis of which I can at least attempt to identify myself, or allow others to try the same.

The name "France" and the adjective "French" would thus carry a great privilege, for the word *frank*, as name of the people and as adjective, was generously endowed with the senses of independence and nonallegiance; the *frank*, capitalized or not, would be the very name of what an identity requires: not first of all its attributes but the frank disposition of its status, and hence the frankness of its declaration. One could say: Identity is necessarily a *franchise* in both senses of the word (exemption and veracity).[2] And this twofold aspect of *franchise* immediately opens identity as such: that is to say in its difference to itself and to the rest. From the distance wherein I affranchised myself, I frankly say that I hold myself there. Thus a relation [*rapport*] can open.

This privilege, of course, is shared with many other names of peoples who designate themselves as "the free" or else as "the people," absolutely, or even as "humans." There is no law, but there is perhaps a tendency by which groups like to identify themselves tendentiously as identity itself, as absolute.

In the case of France, it is interesting that the names of the nation and of the people have perpetuated—along with the entire semantics of "frank" in the French language, of which I have given a few examples, and which spread to names of cities ("Villefranche") or to dispositions like the "*franchises*" of the early universities—this twofold sense of exemption and veracity attributed to the Franks (that is, that the Franks attributed to themselves). The Franks were Germanic, according to the protohistorical taxonomies. Later on—during the age of nationalisms—some French people resented that and attempted to twist history so as to clearly identify France as non-Germanic (going so far as to search for a detour via Troy and Aeneas, in order to find a less barbaric origin).[3]

5

ABSOLUTE

Two axioms:

> Identity relies both on itself and on a lineage. More exactly: It is itself its own lineage.
>
> Identity demands a name.

Identity is in its lineage, for it can give itself only in a gesture that relates the same to itself: "I am I" does not produce such a relation. At most it is the relation of logical identity: "I = I."[1] What is immediately troubling in this equality is that it equally states that all the "I" are identically "I." "I" cannot be posited like an *x* identical to *x*, because the "I," the very word itself, has already engaged the process of its identification. It will speak—or do something—that *will be* its identity. (This is already done the first time the child says "I," or when he or she designates himself or herself by name.) However, in order to do this, he or she must return in himself or herself to a point prior [*en amont*] to himself or herself: to a point where, for instance, prior to any speech, he or she was already disposed to speak. But this is still too general: It is a return, a Platonic anamnesis that would not only be a return to the true Forms (or "Ideas") but rather to *the* singular and proper form of this "I." And this form is deposited nowhere, it is not given, it is not given to him or her: He or she gives himself or herself to it, or gives it to himself or herself, which amounts to the same, and he or she does so by identifying himself or herself.

Supposing that there is no concrete, identified lineage, it is in any case from the outset caught in this lineage or delineation: from self to self, from same to same: "Become what you are!" This is very well said: You are not what you are; you have to become it; and nothing is given to you for this purpose since what you are is nowhere but at the end of your becoming. And at that point, you will not be there anymore. And yet, as you know, a line is stretched from the first absence to the last, a line of existence that is properly yours, absolutely, exclusively.

How can I avoid mentioning this: I am writing these lines a few days after the Swiss vote that forbade the construction of new minarets[2]—there were only four—on the Helvetic territory. I tell myself, mischievously: Switzerland identifies with its bell towers, with all the peaks and needles of its imposing mountains, perhaps also with its *alpenstock*, maybe even with William Tell's pointed hat and the apple on the head of the son; that is enough for it, enough heights, enough raised fingers toward the sky. Let us remain among ourselves with our sublimities. Switzerland strikes a terrible blow against its own identity: It closes it off; it locks it through a gesture that vindicates—out loud or under its breath—little more than what I just said.

Switzerland is not alone in this, although at present it is displaying the most spectacular retreat into an identity that above all need not become what it is because it already is it, and knows it; it already is and has what it is, and it has within itself and for itself, safe from any Islamic outgrowth, an accomplished plenitude.

But if an identity realizes itself in and as the movement through which it goes toward what it will never be able to reduce to the identical, or, to put it differently, if a true identity is not an identity *in itself* but an identity *for itself*, this means that no identity "in itself" is ever given—neither in an embryo nor in someone dying, "such as in himself at last . . . ," nor in a man or a woman at the height of their expression—and it means that identity is always the being for itself that makes and welcomes what it has no reason to presuppose as "its own" but which becomes it because that very one—the "one who identifies"—makes it its own.

And democratic politics means only one thing: that for any possibility of identity (personal, collective, the two together, this too is not given in itself) a space be opened in which to trace, unfold, ramify its line(s) of identification.

This is indeed why identity demands the name, for the name carries infinitely more than what the civil status, for its part, assigns to it. Civil status is only the identification *in itself* of what the name bears, declares, addresses *for itself*. That is to say, a height of sense—a height or a void. We know that a proper name does not have a signification, that its meaning is precisely only that absolute "proper" in relation to which all kinds of properties, attributes, qualities, are external.

The name designates the proper, not the property—and not the essential property—of the individual or the group (once again, let's not separate these too much), but quite exactly the proper in the sense in which existence is not a substance with qualities but an act of being that qualifies, in a singular manner, all the attributions, circumstances, and relations in which it is engaged. Such is identity: It qualifies all the determinations that fall to it as being "its own." This does not mean that they "belong" to it, but that they find themselves in relation to the "idem" of the identical, to its sameness.

The *idem* is absolute: It is not the same as this or that other; it is the same as itself. Separated from everything: *ab-solutum*. The sameness that identity puts into play is a sameness that does not amount to the same [*même*], because it "itself" [*lui-même*] is not given, and will never be so definitively. One could say that identity accomplishes the eternal return of the same of which Nietzsche spoke: a return that is not a reprise, a reiteration, but an infinite return to the absolutely different whose sameness is made up of this absolute difference.

Who, then, could speak of identity—of a person or of a people? From the outside, one can capture only features that are distinctive, interesting, important, but which will never be able to give access to the *idem*. From within, one can have a great talent for introspection, but the first and last knowledge remains this: that there is nothing to know. Nothing, if not some "one." This "one" remains indubitable, but its absolute unity vanishes in the infinitesimal point of its provenance and destination. "*Ignore thyself*!"[3]

What constitutes, with respect to identity, a great writer? It is that one can never claim to have discovered the ultimate identity of their characters. Think of James, Proust, and Faulkner. A bad writer, on the contrary, already has, laid out before beginning, identified identities.

6

WHO?

The government's proposal of a debate or a consultation on "French identity" meets up with one consensus and gives rise to yet another. The first is the consensus of modes of thought attached to the distinction of a national reality as generic, native, or natal—according to the origin of the word "nation"—of that consistent, if not substantial, community that the population of a country is supposed to constitute, whether this reality is represented as nature or spirit (which, in the end, makes little difference). The second is the consensus of a way of thinking that has long been educated in "cosmopolitanism" and in the "international"—terms that should not be reduced to their historical connotations, for these thoughts are born with the consciousness that humanity is multiply identical to itself and, to say it in a word, that there are no longer any "savages," without this making it possible to determine any better what the "civilized" person is.

I agree with neither of these. "To be French" is not for me an empty expression, but I always hear something of the call "proletarians of all countries . . . ." (especially since we know much better than Marx how the super-rich of all countries are as thick as thieves).

"Identity" does indicate to us a property of being, but I do not forget that "I is another," and this other is also in being.

The belonging to one form or another of community (whatever one puts under that name), perhaps even the simultaneous belonging to several communities, is indeed given with birth, which does not mean that it is a mere unchanging constraint. It is an occasion and an accident: Two words to say that one "falls" *there*, for the very simple reason that one cannot fall nowhere, which would make no sense. On the contrary, it is in this fortuitous, unpredictable *there* that a tracing of sense can begin.

Furthermore, the belonging to this original community thereby delineates the edges, at least—the more or less proximate and tangible borders—of other communities and the possibility of going from one to the other, perhaps of choosing another one, or several others, or even none. A twofold principle of falling and plasticity: This is how what one calls an "identity" announces itself: Whether it is approached as personal or as national changes very little since the two are intertwined and can either support or undo each other.

It is therefore not a question here of embracing either slogan: "identity!" or "nonidentity!" (or a mixture, melee, or process, as you will). It is a question of entering into the gap and dehiscence that an identity opens of itself within itself.

Identity is the landing point—or the point of inscription, one might say—whence a path can begin to be traced out.

By definition, the point has no dimension. The path [*le tracé*], for its part, can open the furthest, most circumvented, entangled, even murky ways. But it is always traced starting from the point, traced from that same point. A point and a labyrinth, such is the secret of an identity. From one to the other, there is permanent contact and permanent dehiscence. One is then bound to lose oneself in one or the other. Surely, one does not lack a few markers which indicate a continuity and which allow one to speak of an "identity"—although it is understood a priori that one could never reduce the infinitesimal character of the point or the rigorously unfigurable character of the path.

These are basic truths, which we know as long as we pay attention to all that proliferates around the question "who?"

For instance, who were the Salian Franks? All it takes is a different intonation to shift from a request for information (dates, places, customs of this people) toward a questioning of being—but who were they, in truth? How can we understand them? Where was the heart or core of their identity? One shifts from a question of the data used for identification to a question of identity.

Who—another example—raises the question of French identity? Who is the one who does this? I am not speaking here only of a name, but of a cabinet minister, a government, a movement (which by the way appears to be troubled, embarrassed, and hesitant about its own initiative). Who is to be found there? Is it already the national identity itself? How did it identify itself? By the fact of occupying the executive power? But does power have ultimate control over identity? It does have some maps for that, without speaking of other coordinates, imprints, images. But is that more than mere identificatory data?

Now, if each French person is a "who," like any other human subject, and if this "who" could never be reduced to a "what," France itself is another kind of "who," irreducible to any characteristics (population, situation, GNP, wines, cheese, and airplanes). And what complicates matters is that each "who" of each French person includes something of the "who" of France, and reciprocally. However, one does not access this extremely remote zone where the various "who's" emerge, slide, multiply, where I am French but also something else (who knows? partly German, partly dog, partly stateless, partly ocean lapping at the dune); one never accesses this vanishing point, this point of infinite gathering and dispersion. One also does not access the zone that is much deeper than Lutece, Bibracte, and Karlsruhe where ways of speaking, gestures, signs and insignias, desires and appearances foment unawares new ways of being a people, a population, and a community.

7

WHY SPEAK OF IDENTITY?

For anyone who works in what is called the "social sciences," for a historian, a sociologist, an ethnologist, a psychologist, or a psychoanalyst, for a theoretician of literature or art, but also for an artist or a writer, and for a philosopher, the announcement of a debate on national identity could at first provoke only an outburst of incredulous laughter. What! All of a sudden we are to have a debate on three notions at once—identity, national, national identity—the complexities of which, the difficulties, at times the aporias or the dangers, but also the constant limitations as well as the constant opportunities presented to the ambivalence of the imaginary, have never ceased for the last forty years to be the object of intense and fecund research—including, let us mention in passing, the work of one of its greatest representatives who has just passed on, Claude Lévi-Strauss, respected by all. It is not difficult to imagine what he would have thought of this debate.

I am not expressing here the ill humor of an intellectual guild. What I am saying is that what two generations of scientists, thinkers, and artists have chosen as a privileged field of research—the relativity of "identities," the intertwined lacing of this notion with an internal difference, the impossibility of assigning unbreakable identities to a "territory" or to a "culture," to a "person" or to a "language," or, in the end, to something like a "sense" or to the position of a particle—all of this did not arise from mere phantasms or speculations.

Identity has since long ago never ceased to be wounded, bruised, or simply transformed, displaced, disfigured, or transfigured, perhaps simply metamorphosed: simply and abysmally. Perhaps one should say that the industrial revolution, bourgeois democracy, and changes brought by digital technologies have more than anything displaced identity: that of social roles, family roles, belonging to communities (local, familial, religious), and finally that of "nationality," which began as an emancipation from foreign tyrannies but ended up in imaginary or even mythological fixations. Fascisms were nothing other than a hypertrophy of identities inflated with the very idea, an empty one, of identity. Into this idea it was possible to throw anything and everything, all mixed up: blood and soil, terror and mirage, military ambitions, symbols of all kinds, annexations, a new order.

And now it is an even more preposterous catchall that we are presented with: One tosses together national, even "ethnic," motifs, religious symbols (devoid of any theology), rewritings or readjustments of "human rights," fervent calls to a history already grown old, various tricks to make sure that the judiciary and even legislative branch do not overly disrupt the action of an executive branch that is in all the more of a hurry since it is, as it were, chased by its own identity. It was on the basis of this identity that it got elected; it is accountable for this identity if it wants to maintain a hold on power. And it does want this, since it is by holding power that it identifies itself—itself, in person, and through it the ensemble of interests that it seeks to serve (those interests, in the final analysis, care very little about identity or identities: They require only that a dollar be a dollar, identical to every other dollar but without any other identity). I would stress that these lines do not merely encrypt the name of Nicolas Sarkozy but could apply perfectly well to many others, Ahmadinejad, for instance, or Netanyahu, Karzai, Putin, and so on.

No, the work of thought around identity—that is to say, of course, by obligatory corollary, also around difference—was no intellectual fad: It took up what European culture had just challenged. This was a series of identities all interconnected and of a piece, the identity of man, of woman, of the animal, of God, of a rational order founded on a "principle of identity," and the identity, finally, of that Europe that had never so clearly identified itself—distinguished itself from others and recognized itself—as when it had not yet propagated within itself that desire for "nationalities," and as long as it thought it possible to impose itself on the world as the identity, by definition unique, of civilization *itself*.

Truthfully, ever since the twentieth century, it is identity as such in all of its aspects that is put into question: Either it can no longer find itself (this is the archetypal case of the European), or it wonders exactly what it is or can be built on (Saudi identity, Algerian, Malay, Mauritanian, among a hundred other examples of names bearing strong marks of identity but whose figures are hard to delineate). In fact, we are all in the same boat: We are floating on an ocean of identity-forming materials that nothing seems any longer to be able to crystallize into "identities"—which, moreover, need not be national, and which could include nation and culture, religion, art, and language.

It is only to that extent, furthermore, that we are constrained to speak of "identity." In the past, one was Kanak or Cossack, Berber or Breton, French or English, English or Scottish, and one belonged to that parish, synagogue, or mosque, and that group, lineage, totem, island, or valley. One did not speak of identity because it was indicated by signs. One speaks of it when there are no longer signs, or when they no longer refer to anything.

8

PEOPLES

The question of cultural identities is a very serious and long-standing one. Let us call them "cultural identities," although we could also speak of "peoples," "symbolic configurations," "languages," "mentalities," and "structures": We could merge all these terms into one—which in fact would be the one that, for a very long time, has carried this complex, indeed overwhelming, value, namely the word "people"; but its current misuses require that we not excessively rely on it. One should hear in it at once the senses of "tribe" [*peuplade*], "population," and "settlement" [*peuplement*], while avoiding the overidentifying rigidity that the word "ethnicity" has occasioned.

A people—to use this word once, nonetheless, in this sense that is both precise and profuse—is nothing other than what corresponds to the principle of nongenerality. Nothing general exists, even if there are general rules, which, for their part, are not existents. What exists is singular, and no doubt Western culture is the only one that has gone through the episode of a discussion of the existence of "universals": This was not an accident; it had to produce the necessary distinctions to be able to handle objects of science as distinguished from objects of perception. But we could show that, even for those who maintained the existence of "universals" (qualities or real properties), these existences were no less singular in their own way. As for the existence of God, it goes without saying that even though it includes the whole of possible universalities, generalities, and particularities, it can only be—if it is—the most singular existence possible.

Everything passes through divisions, classifications, distinctions, even the great "kingdoms": Minerals have their classifications, orders, families, and so on. This is all the more the case for plants and animals—until they are replaced or set aside, for better or for worse, by these other ways of existing that our technology produces and which begin to complicate, modify, and change our human identity.

However, there is never, neither in nature nor in technology—as long as they can be distinguished—a pure individual. Everything begins with the species, not with the individual. This is not a matter for paleontology but for ontology *tout court*:[1] Being is plural or it is not, and it is so in all the registers of being. Humanity does not begin with an original couple, but with a group, and as a group. Or better, no doubt, as several groups (which, furthermore, may not have all been "human" in the sense that we know). This already forms the law of existences in general: Plurality and relation, without which one could not even see what "to exist" could mean, apply, if one can put it thus, in a double manner to those existents whose distinctive feature is to belong to the element of sense, that is, to belong to it entirely and expressly: There is no human conduct or behavior that does not "make sense," and furthermore, there is no conduct or behavior of other existents that do not somehow "make sense" in the words, the hands, the eyes of humans, and in—and as—the multiplicity of their productions and exchanges. (The notion that "to make sense" also implies the undoing and unmaking, perhaps even the devastation of the element of sense, is something I cannot dwell on here.)

There are thus first several peoples, several languages, several symbolic and physical dispositions (ways of emitting sounds, for instance, ways of being together, etc.). I am not competent to discuss whether these are many or few. I note only this: There is always one form of people or another, and thus of belonging to a people, or to several, for it is not excluded that one moves around, mixes with others, and so on. At the same time, a people is never originary, neither for itself nor for others. The very fact of peoples pluralizes any notion of origin, and from the outset opens onto a more than originary profusion: that of existence.

In this sense, a people is nothing other than the realization of the symbolic *partage*, the dividing up and sharing out of the symbolic field. We symbolize—we make sense—and this supposes that we share sense but also that sense distinguishes us: "We" are an "us"—if one can put it thus—or we are "between us," as the condition of an exchange of sense, *and* we significantly distinguish ourselves from others "between us." We declare "ourselves" as a space and order of sharing.[2] There can be only a plurality of spaces and orders of this kind. Not only several "peoples," but several ways of "being or making up a people" [*faire peuple*] or of "declaring oneself." Thus the people of the United States have made themselves—literally *declared* themselves—on the basis of a very short history and against a cultural background that mixed European populations that had for a long time identified themselves in very different ways (Germans, Dutch, French, etc.). In sum, its culture was from the outset that "nature" produced by the Enlightenment ("the Laws of Nature and of Nature's God," as the Declaration of Independence says). In a very different way, one could say that there has tended to be, or that there could have been, despite the artificial national construction, a Yugoslavian people—which demands for identity have since dismantled. How many people in Africa have been or still are subjected simultaneously to inherited genealogies and to badly managed colonial divisions and shaky national constructions? And what should we say about Latin America and the widely diverse combinations that played out between Indigenous peoples, Europeans, and African slaves? Or what answer could we give to this question: How many Chinese peoples are there?

In reality, peoples are never completely identifiable, neither in an origin nor in a univocal characteristic, not even linguistic. Peoples are not entities: They are indefinitely exchanged—and changing—signs of our common existence, which itself cannot be gathered under any identifiable "humanity."

9

NATIONS

Of course, at a given time or epoch, there is in each case something of a people [*du peuple*] that has been constituted in one way or another, one that speaks Basque or Finnish, which counts the days or knits their clothes in such and such a way. However, behind this people, its language, its customs [*coutumes*], or stitching [*couture*], there are always other peoples and other languages, other ways, other inventions.

And, of course, each people has an identity, or rather *is* an identity, for one cannot own an identity. In fact, this is how a people becomes a people, that is to say, relates to itself: It "understands itself"; it does not speak its language without innervating it with what one calls a "linguistic sentiment" (and we know, that bilingualism is not always a simple matter); it shares and partakes in more concealed features that include the relation to death or the various modes of singing.

It relates to itself: One understands that this does mean that it relates a people *x* to a people *x* supposedly given before it. It means that by marking out those choices—of sounds, gestures, colors, practices, emotions—it makes "itself": It brings out an identity that becomes recognizable or identifiable to it at the same time that it becomes so to others precisely in order to distinguish "itself." In order to differentiate itself—first, from nothing: from the void, from abandoned being—and, in difference, to open a possibility of sense.

Another possibility: not because it would be better to augment these possibilities, which in a way probably cannot be augmented (so many cultures are buried, forgotten; so many others will be, including ours). But because the sense of sense is its beginning anew, its reinvention.[1] This is why it is often unfortunate to hear celebrated over and over a "multiculturality" that a "progressive" discourse praises as some Dionysiac innovation, when in fact this poor and heavy term was only coined in order to keep together various patchworks whose pieces most often remain, despite everything, caught in the monocultures from which they originate.

"Multiculturality" is the condition of *each* culture. But each one is a point of departure and a send-off, also a kind of drawing, a style, a turn, or a twist, a more or less durable configuration lent to what, of itself, has no figure but that is revealed in its new and unheard of aspects by this turn, this sketching out.

At least one can think that this was the case in Europe, in Africa, in Asia, and in Oceania until there emerged something, now irrefutable, which is much less, in the end, the expansion of a unique model (although it does exist, fast-food, manga, blogs) than the fact that this "model" barely is one. It brings together not the features of a "culture" but those of a *habitus*. What the Westernization of the world has propagated is a habitus or an ensemble of habitus. The latter is without a culture, which also means without lineage and without people.

To this habitus belongs the "nation" in the modern sense of the term, that is, the people that defines itself as a common (or "general") will and which institutes itself as the operator of a common purpose. The "common" can be conceived as the result of a will or on the contrary as produced by a history—the first conception refers to Rousseau and the spirit of 1789, the second to that of the several "nationalistic" movements of the nineteenth century, in particular in Germany.[2] But through these two ways one enters into the movement of a constituting power, with the state being what is constituted.

In a sense, then, the nation is the people itself as a constituting power. At the same time, nations have also undone peoples. There is no doubt that the European invention of the nation-state has blurred at least two types of identity: that of the people as I have described it, which is that of the identity that makes itself by searching for itself and inventing itself, and that of an entirely different order—the identity of the recognizable or identifiable [*repérable*]. We have a name for this: civil status. The registers of the civil status in the proper sense, and the associated multitude of identification and localization papers, certifications of employment, of unemployment, of education—all of this pertains to identity in the sense of the recognizable: the point of intersection, which, to be sure, has no more dimension than the infinitesimal point I have spoken of, the one from which and to which a singular path whose deciphering can only be infinite always returns: an existence.

It is not a question of drawing a Manichean picture portraying the nation against the people. And it is certainly not a Frenchman who should denigrate or denounce what a very remarkable constancy—which did emanate from a people, in some ways—was able to do from Philippe le Bel to Robespierre, and even, let's be excessive, through our two Napoleons, and then Gambetta and Jaures: a few names that punctuate the history of a people (still the one bearing the name of the Franks) that reduced and annexed a few other peoples (Occitans, Toulousains, Basques, Bourguignons, Normans, Alsatians, Corsicans) through a mechanics of wars and alliances that at the same time did not prevent an identity from being formed—oftentimes under duress—and what duress!—but in such a way that there was also something like the germination of a lineage: one that allows us to draw up the great tableau of France with its cathedrals, its mountains, its Condorcets, and its Hugos.

Yet, at the same time, in France and everywhere around it, it was the culture of the state and of industry that quietly, without anyone really noticing it, was displacing the deepest logic of peoples and identities. The peoples having become nations—identified with them or absorbed into them—were becoming less capable of these new beginnings, of these inventions that had produced and renewed their characteristics. The ground was becoming less hospitable for "landing points" from which to create and trace new paths. We are rather between recognizable reference points [*points de repère*]: Civil status and the admission to civil status, or citizenship, have become the sole virtues and at bottom the sole true "identities" expected of anyone, any group or individual, and, between these highly regulated reference points, the trajectories are given by the needs, opportunities, and—if possible—the auto-regulations of society.

The latter is neither a nation, nor a people, nor a state, nor a group, nor individuals. Its name says it quite clearly: Society associates, but it does not identify, except with civil status, social security, and every type of coding. But coding is not an identity. This is obvious. And yet it is to "society" that the proposal or the demand was made to "debate" what identifies it.

Many of those who were asked to identify French identity would be more than happy to share a "country" [*pays*]—which is another name for identity, as that "country," sometimes called a *bled*, which often remains for them an "elsewhere" from which one has departed and to which one will perhaps not return.[3] They would like it if what is "here" could also become a country in this sense: But we see that it is not a country; it is a society, an administration; it is a functioning system. It is not a life; it has no identity; it cuts its being into small pieces: bell towers, vineyards, tribunals, human rights (ah, humanity! but what is that?), secularism, the inner cities. . . . Where is the country, they ask? Where are the people? We answer them with "identity."

In addition to the fact that this is a decision by the state, which the prefects are ordered to implement, and which was presented as a grand and beautiful national initiative concerning the nation itself, the task of restoring the identity of France has been given over to a kind of journalistic psycho-sociology, something like an expanded person-on-the-street interview. As if we did not suffer enough from the countless psycho-demo-culturo-politico-logical mirrors that books and magazines hold up to us every day.

The real answer is on the contrary: No, one does not judge "national identity" according to the standards of a "debate"; rather one modulates that identity in the simplest manner and in the way best suited to the contemporary and future needs of society (for in this respect it is society that is at stake); at the same time, one engages a completely different politics toward the deep causes of immigration. Then one will be able to see the identity or identities that will be formed, the French people or peoples—and why only French? Why couldn't other names appear?

And the basis of this answer is not that the debate of opinions and the psycho-sociology that leaves a stain would be poor or weak knowledge—which they also are. But above all, we are not on the level of knowledge—whether scholarly or not. It is not an issue of acquiring the knowledge of this identity (French, German, Italian, etc.). An identity is an act or a tension whose effects can be recognized but whose nature cannot be isolated like a chemical element.

10

EMPIRES

One will ask: Where are peoples before or outside of nations? They are either in nature—an expression which today cannot have any other sense than that of the figurative sense of "lost, out of place," since indeed there is no forest or steppe that is not more or less subject to administration—or in empires. I will not venture an analysis of "empire"—is there even only one, one unique essence?—nor do I wish to claim that it would be a way of preserving peoples.[1] I note only, with respect to what occupies us here, that an empire is of course identified by its *imperium* (its emperor, its dynasty) but that no search for an identity in the form of subjectivity, as it is sought by the nation, proceeds from it.

It is our task to at least overcome or displace the covering over to which we are accustomed between "subjective" identity, in the sense that I just suggested (people, culture, and community), and "objective," that is, political, identity. This covering over, which we obscurely associate with the general idea of democracy, leads both to the unrepentant and vaguely magical or soteriological usage of "politics" as the taking on of sense or of existence and to the theocratic affirmations that, for their part, have the entirely seductive force of a proposition of integral, politico-religious identity.

11

IDENTITIES, INTIMACIES

No, identity cannot be isolated as a precipitate. It has instead always been, whether for a people or for a person, a simple index—the index of a name—directed toward what comes, and never ceases to come, what comes back and transforms itself, opens new paths, leaves traces, but never a thing or a unity of sense. Identity comes from infinitely far, since it comes from before any possible identification—resemblances, yes, at times appear through the play of kinships, but they only confirm the infinite withdrawal, in each of us, of the point of distinction. Twins know this. In a general manner, an identity that would be capable of identifying itself would collapse into madness. We are aware of pathologies suffered by twins, of paranoias of saturated identification.

The appropriation of identity cannot be an act of possession, nor that of a good that I could seize, nor that of a good that I would receive. Only the identities of leaders [*chefs*] pertain more or less to the two cases. But the leader is no longer the person, nor the people: Rather, the leader is the placeholder of that which can be neither shown nor appropriated.

It is a matter of appropriation. Identity is the appropriating event of some "one" (personal or collective). Such an event does not happen once but constantly, each time. And each time this appropriation forms an "exappropriation," to use Derrida's expression, since there is never an established subject, already identified, to whom the appropriation would return. Each time that subject is different, from others as well as from itself, that is to say, different from any identity. This does not mean that it is highly unstable, inconsistent, and essentially mutable. But the true consistency of a subject is the overcoming at every moment of its identifiable identity. For the subject, its identity is always *interior intimo suo*.

Identity is more intimate—for each one and for the group—than any accumulation of identity traits. France does not know from what unfathomable intimacy (or intimacies) its hexagon,[1] its language, its customs, the tones of its painters or its musicians came. But France also does not know in what new intimacy it could find itself, perhaps already finds itself with—why not?—other configurations, other idioms, other ways that are all themselves touched and shaken in their intimacy.

France—but who, quite frankly?

NOTES

0. FRAGMENTS

1. Then French President Nicolas Sarkozy decided in 2009 to organize a "debate" on the question of "national identity." This "debate" was associated with the goal of reaffirming the values of national French identity.—Trans. http://www.lemonde.fr/politique/article/2009/11/12/le-debat-sur-l-identite-nationale-est-necessaire-selon-sarkozy_1266493_823448.html#ens_id=1258775.

2. While I was writing down these notes, the petition for the suppression of the "Ministry of National Identity," which I signed, was launched. [The date was December 4, 2009. This ministry was dissolved November 14, 2010.—Trans.]

1. CAUSES AND CONSEQUENCES

1. The immigrants.—Trans.

2. *GROS ROUGE*

1. The expression "*gros rouge*"—literally, a thick red—refers to a cheap red wine. This expression has become a symbol for a certain French identity.—Trans.

2. For instance in *Le Monde*, December 3, 2009, 11.

3. Roland Barthes, *Mythologies*, trans. Annette Lavers (New York: Hill and Wang, 1972), 59.

3. IDENTITY IS NOT A FIGURE

1. *Beur* is the term used for French-born descendants of North Africans. *Reubeu* is this term in "verlan," a slang form of speech in French that inverts the syllables of words. *Beur* itself is the verlan version of *Arabe*.—Trans.

2. Marc Crépon has analyzed the philosophical history of these typologies in *Géographies de l'esprit* (Paris: Payot, 1996).

4. FRANKLY

1. A *franc-bourgeois* designates a commoner who in the Middle Ages was exempt from taxes.—Trans.

2. I venture here to write "veracity" and not only "sincerity," for the latter is a *franchise* that cannot easily be freed [*affranchie*] from conditions that are diverse, and unconscious; but how could I not be truthful [*vérace*] when I affirm that I am, that I exist? This should not be heard as one hears it ordinarily in Descartes. This is not an operation designed to reach certainty, and it is even less an issue of immediately defining this "who am I?" as a "thinking thing." Or rather, the goal is not to establish a paradigm of truth as certainty; instead, all identity declares "I am," and this declaration is a "thought," that is to say, a relation to an outside (felt, willed, imagined, conceived, desired).

3. There perhaps exists (I do not know) and in any case there should exist a study of the semantics of the names of peoples and of the way in which identity proposes or imposes itself in them.

5. ABSOLUTE

1. I do not intend to reconstruct here the history of philosophy, but what I am speaking of is subtended by the immense question of the "I" as it unfolded from Kant to Fichte and Schelling, and to us by way of the "subject of the statement/of enunciation."

2. The vote took place on November 29, 2009.—Trans.

3. Emmanuel Levinas, *Carnets de captivité*, in *Œuvres complètes* (Paris: Grasset, 2009), 1:279.

8. PEOPLES

1. I do not want to dwell here on this order of considerations. Let us simply say, to remain purely allusive, that long chains of reason and long sequences in the history of thought are here implied, in the most rigorous way.

2. See my text

"*Le peuple souverain s'avance*," in *La démocratie à venir: Autour de Jacques Derrida*, ed. Marie-Louise Malet (Paris: Galilée, 2009).

9. NATIONS

1. I know that one should dwell on this a bit. . . . I will do so, in these pages or others.

2. The famous 1882 speech by Renan on the nation can be understood only in the context of the opposition to the theses of Mommsen concerning the legitimacy of annexing Alsace-Lorraine. Further, each in its own way, Alsace and Lorraine have never ceased even today to testify to the difficulty of inscribing a culture (let's use this word, for lack of a better term) in a "national identity." In that same speech, moreover, Renan also declared: "Nations are not eternal. They have begun, and they will end. The European confederation will probably replace them. But such is not the law of the century in which we live." (Text available at http://www.bmlisieux.com/archives/nation01.htm.) Now, precisely, we no longer live in that century, nor in the century that Renan was expecting.

3. *Bled* is an Arabic word meaning interior, countryside, or home village. Its use in colloquial French has derogatory connotations but may be tinged with a kind of affection for the familiar.—Trans.

10. EMPIRES

1. We know that for Michael Hardt and Antonio Negri, "empire" as they understand it has as its correlate and threat the "multitude," whose

concept is opposed to that of "people." To initiate a discussion, one would, of course, have to clearly identify the concepts designated in each case by these words: Perhaps there are some intersections between their "multitude" and the "people" as I am trying to think it. But the more fundamental point is elsewhere: It is in the fact that for them everything remains caught under a "politics" that must always in the final analysis be an integration or a salvation of life as a whole. This is precisely what I believe is important to discuss: See *The Truth of Democracy* (New York: Fordham University Press, 2010), as well as "Finite and Infinite Democracy," in *Democracy in What State?* (New York: Columbia University Press, 2011).

11. IDENTITIES, INTIMACIES

1. The "hexagon" [*l'hexagone*] is one of the ways in which France is designated, in reference to its quasi-geometrical form.—Trans.

COMMONALITIES

TIMOTHY C. CAMPBELL, SERIES EDITOR

Roberto Esposito, *Terms of the Political: Community, Immunity, Biopolitics*. Translated by Rhiannon Noel Welch. Introduction by Vanessa Lemm.

Maurizio Ferraris, *Documentality: Why It Is Necessary to Leave Traces*. Translated by Richard Davies.

Dimitris Vardoulakis, *Sovereignty and Its Other: Toward the Dejustification of Violence*.

Anne Emmanuelle Berger, *The Queer Turn in Feminism: Identities, Sexualities, and the Theater of Gender*. Translated by Catherine Porter.

James D. Lilley, *Common Things: Romance and the Aesthetics of Belonging in Atlantic Modernity*.

Jean-Luc Nancy, *Identity: Fragments, Frankness*. Translated by François Raffoul.

Miguel Vatter, *The Republic of the Living: Biopolitics and the Critique of Civil Society.*

Miguel Vatter, *Between Form and Event: Machiavelli's Theory of Political Freedom.*

Maurizio Ferraris, *Where Are You? An Ontology of the Cell Phone.* Translated by Sarah De Sanctis.

Irving Goh, *The Reject: Community, Politics, and Religion after the Subject.*

Kevin Attell, *Giorgio Agamben: Beyond the Threshold of Deconstruction.*

J. Hillis Miller, *Communities in Fiction.*